Rough Spun to Close Weave

Also by Liam Guilar

The Poet's Confession
I'll Howl before You Bury Me
Lady Godiva and Me

Liam Guilar

Rough Spun
to Close Weave

Acknowledgements

Poems included here have been published, sometimes in slightly altered forms, in *Crannog*, *The SHOp*, *The Stinging Fly*, *Words on the Web* (Ireland), *Shearsman*, *Under the Radar*, *Horizon* (UK), *Blue Dog*, *The Mozzie*, *Eureka Street* (Australia). *Free Verse* (USA) and in the anthologies *Nth Degree*, *New Australian Writing* and *Short and Twisted* (both Australian).
My thanks to the editors of all these publications
and to Stephen Matthews for publishing this collection.

Rough Spun to Close Weave
ISBN 978 1 74027 777 8
Copyright © Liam Guilar 2012
http://ladygodivaandme.blogspot.com.au/

First published 2012
Reprinted 2016

Ginninderra Press
PO Box 3461 Port Adelaide SA 5015
www.ginninderrapress.com.au

Contents

The Bunting Tapes	9
Invitation	10
Anno 787	12
Caedmon? Him?	13
You Again	14
The Dangers of Doing Coffee	15
The River	16
Ghost Fences*	17
The River Journey	20
The Captain's Final Dream	21
This is Not My Life, She Said	24
Rereading Wyatt	25
A Love Story, Perhaps	27
What I Learnt From Watching Television Archaeology	33
The Middle Manager's Song	34
Just Once	35
These Heroics 1	36
The Therapist is Everybody's Favourite Aunt	37
These Heroics 2	39
The Facts of Life	40
Lines on a Young Lady's Photo	41
Presentment of Englishry*	43
My Grandmother's Story	44
Byron in Venice	45
Lancelot, Seeking Perfection, Encounters Guinevere	47
Holding a Line	55
It Goes Like That	56
The Piper's Call	57
L'Esprit de L'Escalier	58
Dislocations	59

After the Funerals	60
Things As They Are	61
Ulysses, Again	62
The Decorator Admires His Predecessor's Work	65
A Craftsman Made These	66
More than a Broken Token Song	67
It Still Turns	70
Talking Nothing to the Stone	71
Shackleton's Grave	79

These words worked the long day Harold died,
when Norman French swept up the slope of Senlac Hill
and English grammar broke and bled into the dusk.
Harold's rotted in his unmarked grave,
but the tattered remnants of his word hoard
still colonise the globe. Linguistic vertigo:
fall and find yourself, there in the shield wall,
beating battleaxe on war-board, chanting
'Out! Out! Out!' as the chain-mailed tide,
    grey as the Channel, flows up the hill.

The Bunting Tapes

(With thanks to Richard Swigg and Don Share)

A northern voice insists we hold to windward.
So late in the season, sleet on the dark,
clothes sodden, fingers swollen
fumbling familiar tasks
the craft shifts and squirms,
battering a hostile sea.

Tired eyes stare for the journey's end.
Easier to turn and run with the tide.
Easier to find a safe haven now.
Easier to wait for a favourable wind.

And when is the wind ever right
for the stars you choose to steer by?

Invitation

Before we crossed the border,
fear imagined searchlights,
machine guns, interrogation,
internment in regret.
But when the time came
not a sentry box
or boom gate
barred our passage.

The owners here don't care
who we pretend to be.
They rent us this spare,
whitewashed space:
a bed, a desk, a window
looking out across a placid bay
to the distant reef
which still holds back
the storm-torn surf.

A track leads to the market
past the multicoloured mini van
with its uniformed surveillance team.
Beneath the trees thrashing in the wind,
women roast coffee in a wok
and laugh at my attempts
to name the fruits that clutter
stalls deserted by the sunset.

While you were sleeping
curled into some private joy,
I watched the fleet of fishing boats
brave the blurred horizon.
Do I have faith in a safe harbour
that makes such journeys possible?

I don't have an answer,
only this conviction:
despite the inquisition
we must face tomorrow,
today is opening like an invitation
so I'll wait here for you to wake
and read it to me.

Anno 787

When we landed your watchman came to us
safe in his customs, fluid in speech. Wearied
we dammed his adjectives with the edge of an axe.

Schooled by the sea's indifference,
by storms, shipwrecks, winter's famine;
lotteries of loss and pain that make a life,
we move amongst your settlements

and leave mind-scrambled scavengers
to burble in the ruins: *why us, what did we do
what god offended to deserve this fate.**

**The Anglo-Saxon Chronicle* for 787 reads, 'In that year came the
first three ships of the Northmen. And the reeve rode towards them,
and he would drive them to the King's tun because he did not know
what they were; and he was killed.'

Caedmon? Him?

Saint Hilda, Abbess Hilda then,
a hard core babe who brooked no lip,
said Caedmon, wipe the cow shit
from your clothes. Give us a song. Not me, he wailed,
you know that I can't play or sing in tune.
Last time I tried, you laughed.
They laughed again. He fled the room.
Snug in the hay he soon began to snore.
Now listen here, said God, who looked like Hilda with a beard,
sing something or I'll boil your bollocks, boy.
So Caedmon sang, and so would you, a boring
tuneless song, devoid of art
and proved that he'd been honest from the start.

You Again

Skinny girls in black are making coffee.
For a moment I thought one of them was you
and the memory of our final conversation
gatecrashed my plate glass morning
like those thugs with bowie knives,
balaclavas, baseball bats, who burst into
the local florist in broad daylight,
then ran off with the Easter eggs.

The Dangers of Doing Coffee

Having proved, beyond a doubt,
communication is impossible,
we stare across the polished silence
like baffled diplomats
whose translators have gone home.

I can hear the muted rumble
as darkness opens underneath us.
The choice; to babble or be silent,
with only loneliness and the desire
to be desired to hold us
staring hopefully at one another?

The River

The roots of trees
splay fingers
cupping silence
over shadows.

Mud caked
grey stones,
dark ringed
water lapped.

Circling flies.
Stem twitching.
Water fumbling
the torn tree stump.

Long-legged skimmer
pausing
on its own reflection.

The river joins the dots
encounters, moves on,
then forgets.

On the strewn beach
men step over tenses.
Silent participants
in downstream worlds
the river cannot see,
their hands build boats
to take them there.

Ghost Fences*

Intro The Skulls Speak

And now your questions force us back to speech.
But do we speak our truth, or resonate to what you'd have us say?
Much is forgotten. Illusions stripped like flesh, desire
…The word rings hollow…desolate, we are all that can remain…
amoral truth, unwelcomed, ripped out of obscurity…
…Strangers to anticipation, prisoners of the present indicative…
the river carries rumours of a presence in the hills.
Fresh skulls bloom beneath their skin. Plant them here,
history's chief crop, like tumours on the river bank…

Ghost Fences 1

…if we stared out, slack jawed, at 'History'
incapable witnesses time polishes to bone.
The space inside the skull echoes the river's susurration
wind in the canopy and the shifting light
splinter mosaics on the water's purling surface.
If this is language then you search out its grammar
poor victim of your own sophistication.
We cannot tell you anything.

Be patient as this polished bone and the cracked skull
fixed on a stick will yield enlightenment?
A belief absurd as mountains dreaming acrobatics.
Insufferable conundrums? Eyes that searched beyond
seeing nothing: ears that strained for sounds
hearing nothing: no eyes, no tongue, no ears
still seeing, hearing, saying nothing.

Futile pilgrim, sifting through the past
in search of meaning. We cannot teach you anything.
You deride our answers: we deny there was a lesson.
Inarticulate in life: our skulls are no less eloquent.

Ghost Fences 2

Conscripted to futility: seasonal witnesses to ownership
we stand guard for a while at the edges of the space
the tribe claims as its own. Obedient to directions
(how can the skulls ask questions of their sanity?)
we outstare time: oblivious to absurdity.

If this landscape could be named, then call it loneliness:
a blunt reminder of your insignificance.
Three bands of colour. Above, the endless
empty blueness of the sky, bleached by the sun.
Between, the ragged stripe of forest green.
Below, the blue-grey lake. And you are nothing
more than windblown dots across its surface.

Behind us in the dark, the platforms wrapped in pungent smoke
If we define a boundary do we keep the terror out?
Or like the firelight create a place, familiar, near,
where children cry, old man tell stories
and bodies writhe together in the corners of the hut?

...slack at the edges, even underneath the moon, the landscape
darkens into distance. We stare: failed antidotes to primal fear:
that sense that everything can fade away, cannot be grasped
or being grasped cannot be held but crumbles, flows,
as permanent as patterns forming on the surface of the lake.
Stake out the skulls to claim this place as yours but
it will not notice when you disappear.

Ghost Fences 3

Remembering nothing: at least we proffer evidence
if you but had the skill to read its signs.
Your studies and your theories make you blind.
The blade cut fades, the domed skulls fall,
we crumble, fading, fertilise the soil.
This needs no exegesis.

The words that echo in the brain pan blur
and fail, but one last thought, before the dust
reclaims us from the stage. Take narrative
as reproductive metaphor. Don't wince:
adopt our level unembarrassed stare and see
your role in life: ensure a fresh supply of skulls.

*A ghost fence is a circle, often of skulls on poles, to keep spirits out.

The River Journey

Grey glacier melting
hurrying downhill
loaded with silt
gouging its impatience
through ice-covered rocks.

The treeline,
and the endless rain
donate another burden.
Brown now,
it plunges
mindless as sex
yearning for the plain
deposits and regathers
before annihilation in the sea.

Shaped and shaper
passing through.

The Captain's Final Dream

1

Too tired to cheer, we saw the harbour lights.
We smelt the city on the off-shore breeze
and in our minds, we'd tied up at the dock
slung seabags over salted, aching shoulders
trudged up the hill to well-lit bars
to spend the evening and the night
in brothels drinking, dancing
telling stories of the long haul out.

We'd braved the storms and fears, the chance of loss,
knowing at the end we'd find a harbour
where fear and storms were colours of a narrative
we'd tell to justify our presence in the bay.
Long evenings drying in the sun, nights
we believed were ours by right of scars
we'd show to prove our stories true;
the way a broken mast commemorates a gale.

Too tired to see the tide turn,
or feel the wind change, till we heard the waves
beating on the wrong side of the hull.
We watched the entrance closing up,
and fall away across our stern
until we couldn't tell the harbour lights from stars.

2

That was so long ago.
I count the time in empty water casks
and biscuit barrels scraped of crumbs.
The sail flaps loose, the men no longer have the strength to row.
The ship leaks green and will not hold her head.
The days repeat themselves, with only names
of those that die to differentiate one from the next.
On the horizon, knife-slit
across the blue sky's throat,
clouds mock us in the shapes of land.

3

If you sail this far, believe me,
we landed on the coast of paradise
green like a definition of that word.
We sailed our long ship up the beach
and those who could collapsed on shining sand
and those who could searched out fresh water.
It tasted like the wine god still denies himself
to prove his virtue.

The people here, though few, have welcomed us.
They smile the way Eve did to comfort Adam
on his first day outside paradise.

The crew repairs our ship
dreaming of the harbour that we missed.
I told them: if you stumble into paradise
give thanks. Don't fortify yourself with God or gold or duty
or claim this place was not your destination.
Accept your circumstance.

They place a hammer in my hands

This is Not My Life, She Said

Conscripted body double in a foreign film,
she cannot read the script, so merely waits.
Marlene Dietrich on a chair, with hat.
Rain beating time upon the windowpane.

There is no street beyond the set for her to watch.
But in the non-existent city,
where some Bogart is heroic once again,
the fake light fades to hint at dusk.

(A car door slams. Down several flights
of ill-lit stairs, sad looking men
loosen their ties. Her posters greet them,
like a mantis in their stale bedsitting rooms.

That knowing smile. Those eyes that haunt
their repetitious dreams. The way cold street light
colours skin upon a threadbare sheet.
The way that she'd unpin her hair.)

The ancient lift clanks to announce: *He's on His way.*
Beneath the inefficient light, the shadows
hint at rooms no one has bothered to define.
Spy story? Or a love affair that's doomed?

(The smell of Gauloise permeates the air.
So, yes, this must be Europe; it looks like wine
inside the glass. The table's laid
for two. Bread, cheese, a knife.)

Or just another bit part in a splatter film?
Her gaze now lingers on the shining blade.
Her technicoloured death may well look faked,
her sense of outrage will be unrehearsed.

Rereading Wyatt

Two angry voices, muddled by the wind
and tangled in the sound of passing cars
How could you something something *him?*
The party's starting up. This could go on for hours.

Thomas Wyatt speaks of Anne Boleyn*
I know it's he, not she who lives,
but while I read both seem to be alive
though Wyatt's hurt, refusing to forgive.

The moon's above the bougainvillea.
Across the road, the party's winding down,
the traffic's gone and distant surf
provides a gentle, but insistent ground.

Young lovers bicker in the dark outside:
You told me that you loved me and you lied,
Her answer's lost but somehow I suspect
it ends, *He is the King, He will not be denied.*

I've never heard words used like this before.
Poetic and creative? No, he's drunk
and hurt and howling in the street:
You f--king c--ting bitching whore,

birthing a version of himself dragged up
his throat and spewed across the night:
a vulnerability he doesn't want to recognise;
a howling rage his words can't organise.

Friends intervene. I still can't hear her voice.
Doors slam and cars accelerate away.
Now Wyatt, left alone, tries to describe
what he saw and felt her execution day.

In a net he says, I tried to catch the wind.
He trapped his own pain raging at her choice:
raw ugliness transformed to something fine.
His poem's magic, lie, distortion, take your pick,
to make art from a wounded angry voice.

*The identification of Anne Boleyn, though popular, is here poetic licence. The female in most of Wyatt's poems could be anyone.

A Love Story, Perhaps

1 The Beginning Felt Like This

At three a.m. the wild boys pinball home,
short skirts, high heels,
tattooing their wake.
Raging voices flay the night
but to be their whipping boy
seems preferable to lying here
waiting for the morning.

No lookout called a warning.
A fragrant archipelago
fills the horizon.
Sea pounding on the reef.
The daunting upward lurch
of wave smashed cliffs.

On the beach alone
a moment's unexpected grace,
before the snuffling predators
infiltrate the moonlight.
The lunacy of braving them
to find you. Changing shape
I entered the garden

2 Lonely Planets

while she undressed. The guidebook
omitted smells/scents/stench of street vendors.
Somehow the imagined landscape
became a list seen from an awkward silence.

The careful traveller takes precautions
before entering this sacred place
do not be impatient or try force
until you're welcome champagne and strawberries
in the honeymoon suite pay attention to the rituals
listening for variations of water
splashing in the shower imagining
hands moving over under in between.

Silence after the water stopped
blank spaces in the guidebook
before the handle turned. Follow the map,

stay away from places marked 'forbidden'
until you know your way around
clumsy exploration often leads to disappointment
do not attempt everything, prioritise.

The phrase book provides words, not understanding
translate replies best you can then dress and leave
the unfamiliar smell hotel body wash anchors the memory
as allowable baggage for the long flight home. No matter
how intense the experience two people leave the room:
visitors with guidebook dreams, phrase book conversations.

3 Binary Opposition Remix

Welcome to the liminal theatre.
Without us, mask, apron,
gloves are fancy dress;
rack, thumbscrew,
boot, museum furniture.

In the cranial arch of this smoke-stained vault,
where the nameless forms go whispering
across these dripping walls,
nothing is forbidden.
Explore the unacceptable.
Relax, there is still time. Our lovers
dreamt of us like this;

a body on the rack or a hand
upon the wheel. The cold air
wrong against my skin, I wake
inside the stinking oubliette
beneath this nightmare:
looking up at me looking down.

A cracked fouled leather glove
drifts along the inside of a thigh,
plays, lovingly, between these legs.
Don't be ashamed if you're aroused.
Once the tearing starts
there will only be reactions.

4 Mr Normal's Lecture On Synecdoche

Mr Normal, in a three-piece suit,
steps out of my mirror,
brushing at the tiny flames
which run along his sleeve.

'It would be a mistake, I think,
though not one that I've made,
to believe that love is all you need,
or to confuse the part for whole.'

He disappears, leaving
smouldering footprints on the carpet.

She, naked, rising, starts to dress.
I am the falling angel,
watching paradise recede,
remembering the garden,
where for once, I felt at home.

5 On a Night When No Dogs Bark

the traffic stills, too early for the drunks,
the sirens distant, the streetlight
fails across the badly painted wall.
Turn down the passage, step from the light,
feet squelching rubbish, fingertip
the bricks and mortar, till your hand
falls off the edge into the night.
Then turn right down the alleyway
which spines the space between the gardens
heading to the park and open sky.
Pass back gates, splintered, weathered,
flaking, hinges rusted, locks untried,
through pools of muted conversation
till you come to where the tree
troubles the darkness, and the blank
of pebble-dash broken by two white
framed windows. Watch the right one
till the light comes on. The blinds are drawn.
A shadow moves, then merges with another.
Hell's gatekeepers, about their business.

6 The Wrong Fairy Tale

Behind each ornate door
a princess waits
to hear the words
that set her free.

As you pass along
the shadowed corridors
dragging your chains
voices call your name
rising and falling like the sea.

Born to the tidal pull of this task
you studied the ritual;
rehearsed the aftermath.

While they perfected themselves:
brushed their hair
practised their songs
waiting for this day.

Now desire prowls on sharpened claws,
but in your mouth
the magic words are wrong.
The doors stay shut.

Step out into sunlight
to the skin tightening kiss
of the cold sea air.
You'll count the pebbles on the beach
before you understand
why your shackles fell away.

What I Learnt From Watching Television Archaeology

We've found another body! Cut
to cleavage shots of fine young animal:
bare shoulders, swinging breasts,
definitely female. Adult, young,
still fertile. On her knees, undressing
bones; the mouth gapes and the skull,
turned sideways, concentrates
upon the probing knife.
Fade in the expert to explain
what is revealed: age
in the worn tooth. A woman,
by her pelvis. Cause of death?
A subject for some further tests.
Linger on the living now,
back in the ditch, tanned flesh,
strong legs. *We learn so much*
about a culture from the way it treats a body.
The way it is displayed for viewing
reveals the truth of what is valued.

The Middle Manager's Song

Something won't forgive
the endless compromise
between what could be
and what is.

Successful? That I am,
in seeking out
a joyless win win
when I can

and dream of Icarus;
the reach beyond the possible,
the burning fall that scours itself
across the viewer's eyes.

Flamboyant? Go to hell.
What must be done
gets done.
I do it well.

But something won't forgive
the endless compromise.

Just Once

On winter evenings coming home,
the fire was my concern.
If it were dead
I'd have to bring it back to life
before my dad's return.

Often the process failed.
The paper burned the wood,
the coke refused to catch.
By the third attempt,
I knew it was no good.

The doorbell and the sound of shoes
scraping on the mat. He'd see
me on my knees, the rubbish in the grate:
You put the kettle on.
Leave this to me.

I'd watch him do what I had done
and see the flame, promisingly frail
grow till the coke was glowing as it should.
Just once. Just once
I'd pray, while making tea
just once, please, let him fail.

These Heroics 1

I envy you, Cuchulain, the simplicities
of your trade; finite as any whore's.
How easy it must be to 'step up to the ford'
and face 'an overwhelming host'.
I know the fear that dries the mouth,
and I have learnt how it refines performance
when technique and habit overcome the urge
to flee. What's there to fear in death
if life has been enjoyed? As metaphor
you're flawed. What do you know?
The father's fear when doctors
can't discover why the child is sick?
You never faced the dole, never
measured out each day not knowing
if you'd won or drawn or lost, when
the only victory you could claim
was to say, I turned up every morning
to face the endless repetitious nothing
of a job. I'll trade you, boy:
your life for mine. We'll see who's hero then.

The Therapist is Everybody's Favourite Aunt

Not the slow one on the farm
who tears the skins from rabbits
in a kitchen full of blood and steam
but the one who gave you sweets
and took you to the zoo
and wondered why you screamed.

No one warned you
that your favourite aunt
objects to walls and cages.
Dressed in her Sunday best
she infiltrates the zoo
to liberate the claws and teeth,
the snarling lust and hunger.
Liberty or death she rages,
not caring whose.

But you've never been so calm.
No really, you've never felt so calm.
She's saying you can speak your truth:
that magic word which will unlock
the princess from her tower
consign the changeling to perdition
and free the true prince from captivity
in some coffee-stained bedsitting room
where a naked beauty, lying on your bed
speculates about your suitability
for the next moon landing. Perhaps
you'll find it next time. You pay her,

calmed, and step outside.
The day is full of razor blades
and the unmistakable sound of a carnivore
free at last, running you down.

These Heroics 2

In the life of any Telemachus there's a moment
(abrupt as a flung spear smashing his chest)
when he knows the stories could be true:
this old man, dozing by the fire,
really did do marvellous things.

The solid ground of his contempt,
which he's been polishing for years,
opens onto doubt and contradictions.

Before the moment ends, if he's no fool,
he won't lament lost strength, rake
the ashes of a reputation or imagine
what Calypso looked like in his bed
but ask, which was the harder, more heroic task:
to burn some foreign town, or raise a son?

The Facts of Life

A mythic landscape talked about in whispers.
The convent girls who giggle on the bus.
Lust, like a slide rule, something you'd encounter
and have explained to you in high school.

Like singing in a foreign language. Obscene
jokes and gestures that you never understood. Words
scrawled on toilet walls. That nameless place
where neck and shoulder meet, the way

a sudden movement turned the world to water.
With Lady Godiva's statue in the rain
teaching anatomy to boys
before nudity was common on TV

Lines on a Young Lady's Photo

For you, it was a normal day,
the day this photograph was taken.
You were having lunch with friends,
after window shopping,
planning what to buy
with next week's pay.

History ignored you with the rest
until you stumbled over him.
Another nondescript face in the bar,
another half-drunk man
fumbling his words, while
talking to your breasts.

But then, a string of accidents
threading the months towards his bed.
November twenty-fifth?
One night of drunken sex,
you left, convinced
the incident was insignificant.

I read his fat biography
to learn the poet was a shiftless git.
The kind of man I wouldn't like to meet
crude, unreliable, and indiscreet.
And there you are, as you were then,
smiling, ruefully.

(You never would afford that dress.)
One face amongst the gallery:
the ones that got away: the ones he screwed;
the ones he wrote those famous letters to.
The spotlight falls on them
where their lives intersect with his,

then lets them age and fade
in someone else's memory.
He wrote a poem about that night.
Famous now, it gets discussed
wherever his work is still read:
six clever stanzas which relate
exactly what he did to you in bed.

Presentment of Englishry*

(Mumchancing it, while the question takes a hike
past dark satanic mills and pleasant (Enclosed) pastures
where we do tug a forelock as m'lady rides to hounds.
Us folks below the stairs do know our place,
stunned in the underground while bombs fall overhead.

We stood our ground at Ethendun, Stamford Bridge and Senlac Hill
then bartered, buggered, battered ground into the soil
from Agincourt to Waterloo; we fell in well-drilled rows
in Somme slime screaming, there is a corner of some foreign
field that is forever foreign. Smashed scorched and sunk
for Drake to Jellicoe. Hatred handed down amongst the people
we defeated, and we reviled by those we did the fighting for.

Prosperity rode misery to market, past sullen tenements
street maggot urchins breeding in the gutters while
the gin-sunk stench of slack jawed women at the gallows
slumping towards oblivion, transported, (not to joy) their men folk
beaten dogs, looking anywhere but up. By what grounds English?
West Midlands, I. Not mercenary, prat, a Mercian! Of Penda's folk?
Gehyrest Pu?) Of course not.

---

*Are you English? *Presentment of Englishry* in the eleventh century was
the offering of proof that a slain person was an Englishman, in order to
escape the fine levied upon hundred or township for the murder of a
Frenchman or Norman. Gehyrest Pu? Do you hear and understand and/
or are you listening?

My Grandmother's Story

We hadn't been there long.
That night, we blew the candles out
said our prayers and went to bed.

Hobnailed boots on cobblestones
in the dark outside the window
heading down the garden to the shed.

There were no cobblestones
outside the window, just an
overgrown, untended flower bed.

But every night: the unmistakable
familiar sounds of hobnails
on the cobbles, heading for the shed.

My dad, he told us not to be so daft.
He hated seeing garden go to waste
so dug, ignoring what the neighbours said.

Beneath the window, down a foot, or less,
he scraped his spade on cobblestones.
Looking up, he saw where they had led.

Well, lord, you can imagine
we didn't sleep that night.
Father was right middling upset.

Even more so when he found
what was beneath the floor boards
in the garden shed.

Byron in Venice

(The poet in exile)

The debris of a city in decline
slops at the crumbling steps,
as the sun sets over palaces
even dusk can't dignify.

The clock strikes, he puts down the page
and calls for servants. Suddenly
cannot remember if he is to meet
the opera singer or the serving maid.

No matter how elaborate the choreography,
his hands run free, his mind completes the rhyme.
Afterwards, duty done, excuses made,
he'll coax these stanzas to their climax

and scrawl defiance on the blank of time's indifference,
graffiti on the walls of history.
He has explored the tangled pathways of his heart
and written travelogues for those who stayed at home.

If that leads here, to age and desolation;
the fading light, broken on the Grand Canal,
where life is repetition, and even lust grows stale;
the boys and women he has loved

the friends he misses as he dines alone,
faded signatures on bundled letters,
locks of hair, old arguments the night returns;
if it leads here; beyond the poem, what remains?

An ageing face, once beautiful,
staring through its own reflection,
soliciting an audience
to dignify the commonplace as art?

Lancelot, Seeking Perfection, Encounters Guinevere

A man convicted of high treason was hung, drawn and quartered.
For the same crime, a woman was burnt.

1

The brutal years build muscle on his arms
but leave his head and heart exposed.
Refine the character, exceed ideals, become
the definition of his age; the man
all men are measured by, the man most women
dream they lie beside. Conscripted as the hero
for an epic tale which runs ahead
drawing the path he has to follow,
what could he ask his world would not allow?

Time happened somewhere else.
Hung in her room, where tapestries
depict dead saints and lovers,
green eyes stab up and in.
Nothing that he's ever learnt
deflects their judgement
when he has retired
to his familiar quarters,
mocking the years of discipline.
What he thought self-denial
was an absence of desire.
He's never wanted anything
except this expertise in death
his peer's respect, the crowd's acclaim
and now her voice creating shadows in his life
whispering his name.

2

The altar candles prove
more is hidden than they can reveal.
His knees on stone, head bowed
the darkness and the ache familiar
as the words he's lost.
A virgin cannot understand
and who is being crucified?
What God of Love denies the act?
He sees their bodies writhing in the Pit.
He sees their bodies writhing in her bed.
Convicted of a guilt he won't accept,
death certain either way,
he gains a vantage point
from which he can survey
walls he cannot leap,
a moat too foul to swim,
but if he'll crawl along the razor's edge
the bridge of swords
might let him in.

3

They'll stuff his genitals into his mouth
choking the sight of his intestines
smoking on the coals.
She reaches underneath his skin
draws out his heart, begins to feed.
He licks the blood that's coursing down her chin
the drips between her breasts
the splashes on her belly, on her thighs.
Mouth locked on mouth as though words
had no place or purpose here
they fall together. Driven
by his desperation
he tries to climb inside, curl up
beneath the refuge of her ribs
deny whatever still divides.

4

She watches from her window,
sees the carters stack the wood
they'd use to burn a guilty queen.
The crowd shoals as the victim's
dragged towards the stake.
This room. This bed.

Behind her she can hear the roaring
flames, of hell or execution makes no odds,
blistering the skin her lover sang about.
Cries of pleasure modulate to cries of pain.
Aren't torturer and lover both the same?
Both shred the public face, unleash
the sweating beast no song can gloss.
Withdrawn behind her gowns
she is the queen again,
to make him be some faithful champion,
not the man whose busy hands and tongue
brought so much joy.

5

The narrative imperative,
illogic of the grail,
which only Galahad escapes:
no matter how elaborate the fuck;
negotiate an aftermath!

Not the familiar strangeness
reentering the everyday
as clothes hung on the floor
hide cooling flesh,
the blinds are drawn
masks are adjusted,
civilities observed,
nor the furtive exit,
from her quarters
lies succeeding lies
facing friends
he has betrayed,
and learning how
to look them in the eyes.

But this essential singularity:
two bodies leave the room
treading their separate paths.

6

To purge the sin that settles like
the stench of bodies burning in the square
he dedicates himself to harsher quests,
to the purity the grail is offering.
He rides on, famished, cold
beyond the mark where other heroes fail.
What good's the world's applause
for what he knows is fraud?

She is the landscape
he would wander through
but to what end, except
participation in the mystery
of repetitious suicide
the frantic fumbling
frenzied flesh to flesh
discovering, as each one falls,
more walls, more ditches,
more locked doors.

The mountains, chapels, grottos
victories; the casual deaths,
the endless miracles all pale.
Not wanting to succeed,
how can he fail?

7

He returns, to claim his prize
to learn, too late,
unlike a castle, gates slammed shut
she can be had, but can't be held.
The treachery of metaphors:
a sleazy go-between
reality and understanding,
having drawn them to the bed,
stoked the flames and hung them
on a fantasy of comprehension
denies responsibility and runs
to sell them for a quarter.

8

Free of impediments,
she turns aside
from futures
they had whispered.

Call it remorse,
guilt, Christian
upbringing;
a lesser man
would call it
a betrayal.

He waves goodbye
and wishes
one last kiss,
which she denies.

Alone, of course, his knees on stone,
head bowed, the ache familiar
as the worlds he's lost.
The candle flames illuminate
smirking icons who deride
the sterile echoes of his prayers
scratching at the gate of Heaven
pleading for a second chance.
Stripped to the clarity of remorse
what's left but dying, devotion
and perfecting his repentance?

Holding a Line

Three hours before, the creeks were rising.
Their brown persistence muttering resentment
at every bridge we crossed. It seemed
far better to go round than risk swift water
ruin for convictions that we did not own.
I choose the longer, unfamiliar way.

Outside the night was liquid noise
battering the windscreen. Wipers futile,
headlights drowning, road smudged
slabs that slid off into murk. And then
the fog and we were lost. Scattered
and irresolute, debating turning back or
pulling over. But not lost to ourselves.
Finding in the heady plunge and slur of
downhill swerve faith in the held line, trust
in the intended journey, commitment to
whatever nerve or skill might get us home.

Improbably lights rushed towards us;
houselights on the valley side that darkening,
hulked up like a tidal wave. One last test
of nerve, a frantic change of gears, an abrupt
unseen turn. Then cold night air sluiced
clean and the pure view clear to the coast.

It Goes Like That

Look, says the fiddler, *we'll give it one last try. It goes like this*!
The dark haired woman at the bar, bare shouldered, tanned
a geometry of curve and fall, is everything that's missing from this tune
which bleeds into a song, so old and raw it should infect the room
with memories of flesh and tears. I sing the solitary girl
who strolls along the riverbank and meets a stranger on the path.
We lay in sport and play/all through the forepart of the night,
but the way he's playing it, you'd think we'd gone to separate rooms
and whiled away the hours with Sudoku. The woman at the bar melts
towards her man. Night loiters in the way his hand drifts up her spine.
Blissful, shut-eyed, she doesn't see him looking straight beyond her
hoping someone else might come walking through the door.
Look, I say, *no, look, look over there. That's how it goes*.

The Piper's Call

(Planxty: Dublin 2005)

The high note, held, stretching
the space above the drone;
like wind torn spray
as the great wave, darkening, builds;
wailing like the curve of the bay,
lean as famine, leaning into
the blurred percussion
of Atlantic rollers, coming home
across unfathomable depth,
to crash onto the present
this cargo of raw, wounded memory.

Like a window blasted open,
the music admits the smell of rain
drumming on the shuttered house.
Where the locals never learn to spell
the migrant's name, the dancers stamp and call,
while by the fire, whiskey and stories
blur in customary gestures.
Laughter and exuberance, suspended
without resolution, above
a strained and ruined loneliness.

L'Esprit de L'Escalier

Before the interview no one had bothered to enquire
what it was like to leave and live abroad.
Lacking an answer polished in a stream of repetitions,
he semaphored absurdities: blue, the quality of light.
The way sand squeaks beneath my shoes.

…he'd woken in a room that should have been familiar
but doors were locked, or leading nowhere, opened
on to emptiness. Portraits in the hall he didn't recognize.
Conversations leaking from the walls made no more sense
than the sound of surf which kept him up at night, or the
birds whose manic laughter brought the light.

He stumbled into dining rooms, the locals smirked,
invited him, laughed at his courtesies. When he
objected to the burnt leftovers they were easily offended.
In bedrooms he discovered lust is not a universal language.

…he had spent time in a ward for the removal
of near terminal nostalgia. For years he stared
at what he'd left behind, until, his masterpiece complete
he wrapped it up and took it home, squinting beneath
a sky that stretched the blue to near transparency
along a beach where the sand squeaked beneath his feet
to a room that should have been familiar.

Dislocations

1

We came across the ocean, towards nightfall
the sunset at our backs stripped colours
from the land. No one was waiting on the quay.

2

…in my case. By coach to Digbeth station.
The terminal stench of City after rain:
damp cloth, upholstery and diesel fumes,
stained our lives and ever after drove us back

again doors hissed contempt, or resignation
and dumped us down amongst discarded ticket stubs.
We struggled through the wash of consonants.
Outside, the only people there without routines,
we could not read the signs.

3

We turned our backs on home:
wind, rain, and sky, the shape of clouds
familiar as an accent calling out

at evening. We landed,
shuffled past the lighted windows,
moved inland, towards sunrise.

After the Funerals

One by one they take their leave; parting
without formal courtesies
startled by the shock, again, as
one by one they take their leave.
Affection, understanding, even knowing
what there was to value, come too late:
gifts delivered past their use by dates.

2

The plane strains upwards in the night, banks, and there,
below the city that we thought we knew;
drab streets, a park, its monuments, some houses
where the welcome meant we didn't want to leave,
revealed as glowing labyrinth: vast, intricate and beautiful.
Too late we realise, again, how much there was to learn
before the detail disappears, becomes a pool of light
shrinking to a faint glow in the skies
behind us as we head towards another dawn.

3

So one by one they leave
stories that I didn't understand and now forget,
lives whittled back to facts and dates
no one contests or verifies.
Box brownie photos in an old shoebox?
Left trying, once again, to reconstruct a map
I never stopped to memorise.

Things As They Are

(Laytown Footbridge, December)

Between the legends of the Liffey and the Boyne
the Nanny slides against the pillars of a railway bridge.
Sliced, furled, folded back against itself, cuts upstream, spins

down past banks of silt where flocks of common sea birds
fossick amongst the dog shit, condoms, broken shells
to meet a sunless, surfless Irish Sea. But

could the resonance of history, or the hand
that drew the Book of Kells, improve the patterns
on the surface of this dirty stream?

Ulysses, Again

(For Tony Thwaites)

1

Mr Leopold Bloom, my dear old friend,
invites me on his peregrinations
through the possibilities of English;
a Cook's Tour, driver one James Joyce.
Polite as ever, we set off once more,
finding where we are, by avoiding
where we really want to be

2

Pronouns renounce fidelity
and start to slide, like guilty lovers
inching closer to the subjects they desire.
Words evade the dictionary;
thumb their noses at Saussure.
This book then is their Eccles Street,
where it's always four p.m.
and Mr Fowler and the OED
are stranded by the fireworks on the beach

3

Meaning doesn't 'recede
down an endless chain of signifiers'
but multiplies like Ebola, spiralling
away through the bloodstream, infecting
everything with potential insignificance.
Time can be measured to a femtosecond;
but no one maps the limits of a connotation

4

Reality revealed: a fractured footbridge
across a flooded Liffey! We totter above
a dirty, roiling, swirl of language,
collapsing, realigning, rejecting fixed or final,
flushing words and phrases in a game of cosmic pooh sticks,
rushing remnants of communication to a distant,
dreaming midnight sea, where mutated offspring
wait to erupt and eat the daylight

5

On O'Connell Bridge, we both looked down,
braving vertigo, while seagulls mimicked syntax,
circling a crumb of sense. So we return,
but never to the Ithaca we left.
Bloom, by candle light, tiptoes through shadows.
Exhausted adulterers, the restless words
still shift, refuse to settle, flicker: my wife,
his lover, Miss Tweedy, Mrs Bloom,
empty clothes, fragrant with the scent of Molly,
upstairs sifting selves. Bloom wants to share his cocoa
but I have miles to go, and promises to keep
so tip my hat, and leave him to his sleep

The Decorator Admires His Predecessor's Work

That's genius that is. You won't find many
can do that today. Do what, she asked
wanting the old-fashioned wallpaper removed.
Craftsmanship. The man who hung that paper
knew his trade. Worked for the thrill of a job
done well. Proud of a skill that proved itself
when no one noticed it. Me, I would give
anything to be that good. And

how long will it take you? Years Missus.
Study, practice, victories, defeats. This job.
Sorry. Two days. First we strip his work
pull down that old stuff, slap on undercoat
than wallop on the paint you chose last night.
I'd like to take the time to do it right,
then both of us could… By the hour?
Quick, Slick and Outta Here. That's me.
Whoever hung this paper loved his work.

A Craftsman Made These

Those fine, skilled fingers,
turned the raw materials,
impatient with the answers
suggested by the metal.
Rejecting the obvious,
refined the mechanisms,
imagined delicate designs,
risked his eyesight
tracing dreams into reality.
So proud of his art
he signed his own name for posterity.

If you dared look closely
would you refuse
to admire the filigree
that ornaments
these thumbscrews?

More than a Broken Token Song

(For the ballad singers, with gratitude and affection)

On a night when the wild wind was raging
Came a knock at the old cottage door
A ghost from her past, who'd come back at last,
A sailor home from the war.

He'd a kitbag slung over one shoulder
Was wearing a fancy new hat,
He'd lost his right leg, so he leant on his peg
And his left sleeve was pinned up and flat.

It's seven long years, said this sailor,
Since I left you and headed to sea.
I've hugged many shores, and kissed many whores
But I knew you were waiting for me.

Round the horn in a storm, we were down to bare poles
Then squashed flat by an eighty-foot sea,
She went down with all hands, but I struggled to land
'Cos I knew you were waiting for me.

When the Bugis men boarded our trader,
Outnumbered one hundred to three,
I gritted my teeth, and I gutted their chief
'Cos I knew you were waiting for me.

He'd wrestled a shark up the Congo,
Been captured by cannibal tribes,
But he'd made his escape from that terrible fate
By offering his leg as a bribe.

He'd been stranded in deserts and jungles,
Been on ships that were crushed by the ice
It came as no shock he'd been stuck on Ayers Rock,
And had been to the moon at least twice.

He'd been lost with Franklin, stranded with Bering
Been cook on the *Marie Celeste*,
Was sunk at Trafalgar, helped burn the Armada
But claimed sailing with Brendan was best.

And so on for fifty-five verses,
Wrecks, pirates and battles and whores
I don't say he lied, but she broke down and cried
When he said, I'm not finished, there's more.

Well you've heard this before I imagine,
And you've guessed how this story should end:
She'll say something silly like, I missed you, Willy,
Then call him her darling again.

But the question you all should be asking
Is who is narrating the story?
Not the man in the gale retelling the tale
To a girl who is bored by his glory.

Seven long years is one hell of a time
(unless you're a nun), to stay chaste,
while he suffered at sea, she had shacked up with me,
for great sex, and my help round the place.

So I watched from where we'd been lying,
I wanted her back in the bed.
I could see his fine hat, so I took aim at that
And blew off the top of his head.

It Still Turns

After torture: dawn.
The birds' undimmed enthusiasm.
In the place of execution,
the martyr's fiery death.

The crowd, confused by anticlimax
disperse to reacquaint themselves
with lives they thought they had
abandoned. A truth worth dying for?
Whores ply their trade,
the thieves and liars prosper
and the children of the poor go hungry.
A king might change his face

beneath the crown God
gets a different set of clothes
and the exuberant birds
will greet the dawn.

Talking Nothing to the Stone

Nothing, like something, happens anywhere.
Phillip Larkin, *I Remember I Remember*

The year 1398 saw one of the greatest anti-climaxes in national history taking place, or rather, not taking place on Coventry's Gosford Green.

Coventry Telegraph

Yet like Lir's children banished to the waters
Our hearts still listen for the landward bells.
John Hewitt *An Irishman in Coventry*

This simple, ugly plaque records that some time in the
   fourteenth century,
the date depends upon which source you use, Bolingbroke and
   Mowbray
didn't fight a duel. My favourite stone, in all that's left of
   Gosford Green,
beside new plastic swings, designed so no child breaks a bone.

Richard, a spineless king, by most accounts, decreed
the fight should stop before it had begun and both men would
   be exiled.
If they came back he'd have their guts for garters, according to
   my dad.
Unable to defend themselves, they left to pace their days out in
   a foreign land,
as I did, twenty years ago. But like Lir's children, banished to
   the waters,
hearts listen for the landward bells. And so I have returned,
to stand here in the winter light and photograph this stone.

I'd like to meet the child who knew this place
as marcher lands to his familiar world.
The swings: where he was Batman in a home-made mask,
or Thor the God of Thunder, who would fly
above the dirty city to a place where bad men schemed
who could be fought, and beaten, hand to hand.
Where victory was proof that god or good was on your side.
and the winner got the gold, the praise, the bride.

Long before he learnt to ride with Arthur and his Knights
and raid along Far Gosford Street,
to loot the city libraries and find another quest
where knowledge was the grail and books, old songs,
a lover for the night, friends for the journey
and a road that never straightened
were all that he desired?

The desire remains, if knocked about.
As Larkin said, *Books are a load of crap*.

Good on yer, Phil, you miserable old sod.
You nailed a city in one damning line,
because no one acknowledged you
because no young girl raced to drop 'er drawers
responding to your non-existent charms.
It's not a poem; it's a metric whine.
Stay on your soddin' train
and get off further down the line.

If there was magic in the city walls
far from the factories and football
you'd find it there. A spiral stair
and high above the other browsers
an alcove where they kept the poetry.
Thank god for city libraries.
From Service and a dream
of Yukon gold, to *Beowulf* and Malory
and that was coming home and there he stayed.
The wandering scholar learnt his trade,
dreaming of study, and of bedding young librarians.

Ah, Gwenhaver.

The pubs had shut, the streets were whispering,
the traffic lights still sent instructions no one saw.
We sat on the old fashioned swings,
the ones you could fall off and hurt yourself.
There was a party, see, she'd gone 'cos she was bored
and she was drunk. I was away. She met a boy,
you know. It started as a joke. Then there were stairs, a bedroom.
She couldn't find the light. An adult's double bed,
so vast the sheets got in their way.
                                                The creaking swings,
An empty double-decker fades towards the morning.

She'd long thought she'd be thinking about nothing else
for weeks, but afterwards, what stayed with her
was when he went to throw away the thing,
she found the switch and saw the patterns on the walls;
tiny roses: red on white: bruises flowering on her skin.

In stories, heroes fall, but being heroes rise,
so Bolingbroke returned, to claim the kingdom.
Like barroom brawlers in those early cowboy films
smashed across the head, they drop, then
rub the noggin, stagger up and carry on.
Out here the ground is hard,
breaks take an age to mend.
So here, perhaps, the road divides,
beside this ugly stump. No knight.
No quest. No trophy bride. No second chance.
Walk home alone, ignore the voice
that's grieving on the phone
pack up your books, guitar, and leave.

While irony is not the only game in town,
feel free, however, to distrust the story.
As I do now in its retelling.
Is it the detail which invites suspicion?
My version of her version of events,
and not of course her 'lover's'.
(Sounds better than 'the drunken git who shagged my ex'.)
Or the parents who returned to find
the buttons from her blouse
and bloodstains on their bed.

His version? Does he wake
beside a wife of twenty years,
and fear if he turns on the light
the paper will be roses: red on white,
The body at his side a girl too stunned to move?
Shirt open, skirt up round her waist?
I doubt it: far too many parties for this Jack the Lad.
Far too many beers. His version: well, I'm at this party right,
I meet this gorgeous Irish bird.
She works there in the library.
Her boyfriend is some poncy student twat
and he's away like, so, she's lonely, see.
She's never done it but she wanted to so bad
we nipped up stairs and did I give 'er one!
I thought her screams would bring the coppers round.
Now who'd d'you think they'll pick for Saturday?
That Spanish bloke is God's own gift!

Or maybe he's a lonely man, who wakes
to stale bedsitter space between his dreams and day.
He sees again her face, the only girl he ever had,
and wonders why he didn't try to make her stay?

Even at this distance, I still hope he rots in hell.

Exactly what took place? Well, Bolingbroke and Mowbray
were armed and ready, there's a clichéd version says that Henry
   had set off.
His lance was levelled, shield gripped tight: he's thundering
   down the lists.
The heralds cry: Hold, Hold, before the spears could splinter.
They dismount, return to cushioned chairs, and wait
for hours until the dodgy king makes up his mind.

What I see now, perhaps, he couldn't.
It's not the nothing Larkin moaned about.
I do remember being interstitial.
Not quite rejected: I grew up over there;
a house with roses rambling up the front
in a road named after Henry Bolingbroke.
Even learnt to speak West Midlands though
dad's brogue, which reappears when I begin to sing,
denies me local authenticity.
If he'd gone home after the war,
I would have sung the old songs in a decent accent,
but my father, and his father, and his father's father
and my mother, and her mother, and her mother's mother,
not one lies buried in the town where they were born.

Movement, away from or towards,
becomes a natural habitat. Trains, planes, boats
libraries or cars: to circumnavigate the globe
to seek new ways of seeing and to see.
It's only exile if you have no curiosity.

(John of Gaunt, if memory serves.)

There is no choice, there's just inheritance
and the sense that comes with taking what you've got.
So sorry, Phil, Old Boy, Old Bean,
that no one recognised the gem that glittered in their midst.
When what you hoped for happens, but to someone else,
does that still count as nothing?
Or is it only nothing when events occur
that aren't the one's you waited for?

So Richard Mowbray went abroad and died,
heart-broken many say. *Ambition should be made of sterner stuff.*
(Another local writer has his two bob's worth.)
Unlike our Henry Bolingbroke, hard man for hard and ugly times,
who did return, within the year, to claim the kingdom as his own.
Richard, captive, paraded through the town where he had sat as judge.
So Fortune and her wheel, in medieval thought, a blind bitch with no loyalties.
So Henry sitting in his cushioned chair, waiting to know if he would die that day.
I wonder if he too came here, to stand alone in failing light,
and contemplate what might have been.
Or did he spit on Coventry as he rode past?

It's far too dark to take a photograph.
What didn't happen seems so overrated:
the girl, the job, the move he never made.
Too busy waiting for the first bus out of here
to notice all the ones queued up to take him home.

I know this place, but wouldn't claim it mine.
Mine is the space between the rising and the falling foot.

Shackleton's Grave

(A Wish)

There will be peace and an end to travelling,
the colour of ocean under a polar sky,
solid as mountains, to bear the brunt
of storms that can no longer trouble
the sleeper in the wind-raked earth.
Time will be glacial, patient as icebergs
where no rumours whisper, no duty calls,
the strong heartbeat of spring and its flowers:
the tides' turn, the snow's fall.

www.ingramcontent.com/pod-product-compliance
Lightning Source LLC
Chambersburg PA
CBHW062149100526
44589CB00014B/1758